PIZZA PARLOR EVANGELISM

REBECCA MANLEY PIPPERT

Rebecca Manley Pippert (M.A., University of Illinois) is a national consultant in evangelism with Inter-Varsity Christian Fellowship and a popular conference speaker. She has also written a book, Out of the Saltshaker and into the World *(IVP).*

Originally published in HIS magazine, the student publication of Inter-Varsity Christian Fellowship. To subscribe write HIS magazine, 5206 Main Street, Downers Grove, Illinois 60515.

InterVarsity Press is the book-publishing division of Inter-Varsity Christian Fellowship, a student movement active on campus at hundreds of universities, colleges and schools of nursing. For information about local and regional activities, write IVCF, 233 Langdon St., Madison, WI 53703.

Distributed in Canada through InterVarsity Press, 860 Denison St., Unit 3, Markham, Ontario L3R 4H1, Canada.

ISBN 0-87784-169-1

Printed in the United States of America

---

14 13 12 11 10 9 8
91 90 89 88 87

Christians and non-Christians have something in common: They are both uptight about evangelism. The common fear of Christians seems to be, "How many people did I offend this week?" They think that they must offend in order to be a good evangelist. A tension begins to build inside. "Should I be sensitive to people and forget about evangelism, or should I blast them with the gospel and forget about their person?" Many Christians choose to be aware of the person but then feel defensive and guilty for not evangelizing. There is something wrong with this concept of evangelism.

Whenever I speak on the topic of evangelism I always sense that people are breathlessly waiting for the new, argumentproof, jelled approach, the magic formula that works on one and all or your money back. But even if I had such a formula to sell, it still would not work. Our problem in evangelism is not that we do not have enough information, it's that *we do not know how to be ourselves.* We have not grasped that it really is okay for us to be who we are when we are with non-Christians, even if we do not have all the answers to their questions or if our knowledge of Scripture is limited. We forget that we are called to be witnesses to what we have seen and know, not to what we do not know. The key is obedience, not a Th.D.

But there is a deeper problem here. Our uneasiness with non-Christians reflects our uneasiness with our own humanity. Because we are not certain about what it means to be human (or spiritual, for that matter), we struggle in relating naturally, humanly, to the world. For example, many of us avoid evangelism for fear that we will offend someone. Yet how often have we told a non-Christian that is why we are hesitating?

I have every right to say, "Look, I'm really excited about sharing with you who God is. But I also know that I hate it when people push 'religion' on me, so if I come on too strong will you tell me?" By saying this I am communicating that we have a great deal in common: I do not want to dump the gospel, and he or she does not want to be dumped on. So on the basis of this common human bond, I am freed to share my faith.

Self-Discovery

God has given me increasing freedom to talk about him to others. But it has not always been that way. I remember, as I reflected on my evangelistic ministry one day as a student, that although I had lots of non-Christian friends, and some had become Christians through my influence, no one had ever become a Christian in my presence. As I pondered why I still felt uncomfortable about evangelism, I discovered several things about myself.

First, I was so afraid of being identified as a religious weirdo or a Jesus freak that I often remained silent when the topic of God came up. How people saw me mattered more than how God did. Ironically, most people respect and respond to a person who has definite ideas and who communicates them clearly rather than someone who seems apologetic and wishy-washy. (We have much to learn from Marxists in their boldness.)

Second, although I saw the needs in the lives of my non-Christian friends, I could not imagine that it was Jesus Christ whom they were really searching for. Jesus was for "religious folk," not for my pagan friends. So because I never really expected them to respond to the gospel, they did not.

Third, I feared that Jesus was just *my* way of life. Wasn't it arrogant to suggest that *my* view was the only way? But as I grew to understand the nature of Christianity, I saw that our faith stands on historical criteria, not just subjective experience. Truth was the issue, not a feeling in my heart. God was not asking me to stand on my own ideas or emotions, but on the very person and work of Jesus Christ. If anyone was guilty of being offensive it was Jesus —not me. It was *his* idea that he was the only way to God, not mine. Realizing this freed me when accused of being narrow. I could answer, "Isn't it amazing that Jesus actually said so many narrow things? Wouldn't it be intriguing to study him to discover why he made such egotistical claims?"

Next, I was paralyzed by fear that I would offend people and forever ruin their chances of entering the kingdom. So I thought, "I'll just be nice and smile and hope they catch on." It is odd but I have noticed that offending people is rarely the problem. If you are sensitive enough to realize it can be a problem, then it is usually not your problem.

Also I could not talk about God in a natural way. I was fine until the topic of "religion" came up.

Suddenly I felt as if I needed to sound "spiritual," and instead of listening, I would panic because I could not remember any Scripture verses. My hands would get clammy; my eyes would dart from side to side hoping no one else was listening; the tone of my voice would change and I would begin talking "religiously." And then I would wonder why they always looked so uncomfortable when we talked about spiritual things! My problem was that I did not think God could be a natural, integrated part of an ongoing discussion about movies, classes, exams or boyfriends. I did not have an integrated Christian world view; God was compartmentalized and separated from "normal" living.

And finally, no one ever became a Christian through me because I never asked them to! Why? Because I was petrified that if I brought someone to the point of becoming a Christian, God would not come through. That would put me in an embarrassing situation so I avoided taking the risk.

Unsuccessful Cover-Up

Then an atheist friend of mine completely amazed me by becoming a Christian. I began to make some startling discoveries when she told me how she had felt before accepting Christ.

"At first I thought, 'Fine, let Becky have her religion—that's her thing. I'm not the least bit interested, but if that's what she likes, then it's all right with me.' When you invited me to dinner, you asked if we could thank God for the food. I thought, 'Oh, how quaint.' Only you didn't just thank him for the food—you thanked him for *me* and our friendship! It made me feel so good. I never thought you felt our relationship had anything to do with God. But then I thought, 'That's ridiculous—thanking someone who doesn't exist for me.'

"Then we went to the Bergman film and afterward you said you'd studied the very same concept that was in the film in your quiet time that day. I never dreamed God would have anything remotely in common with modern cinema! Another day you invited me to an objective, no-strings-attached study of the person of Jesus in the Bible. Fine. Only the trouble was—I really liked the guy! He seemed so real as we would read about him each week.

"But you know what affected me most? All my life I used to think, 'How arrogant for someone to call himself a Christian, to think he's that good.' But then I got to know you—and Becky, you are far from perfect, yet you call yourself a Christian. So my first shock was to discover you make mistakes like I do. But the biggest shock was that you admitted it, when I couldn't. Suddenly I saw that being a Christian didn't mean never failing, but admitting when you've failed. I wanted to keep Christ in a box and let you be religious during Bible studies. But the more you let me inside your life—and the more I knew the real you, with the problems and joys—the more impossible it became to keep the lid on Christianity. Even your admission of weaknesses drove me to him!"

That confession changed my life. What amazed me was that she had seen me in all kinds of circumstances—she had seen the real me—and it gave the gospel *more* power, not less. I had always thought I should cover up my doubts and problems, because if she really knew me she would not become a Christian. But the more real and transparent I was (even with my weaknesses), the more real Jesus Christ became to her.

Now please get this straight. By saying we must be human with each other I am not condoning sin. God's call is to perfection. I am not suggesting we share our weaknesses as if it is a competitive sinning match in order to be real. Sin is not God's brand of humanity; perfect obedience is. But so is humble confession when we fail. So our goal must be to live within the balance of aiming for perfect obedience and complete vulnerability.

Called to Be Human

I had to learn from experience what Scripture teaches in 1 Thessalonians 2:8: to share the gospel we must share our life, our real person. If we do not grasp that Christ has freed us to be authentic, we will see evangelism as a project instead of a lifestyle, and non-Christians more as objects of our evangelism than as authentic persons.

I remember asking a girl once if she felt comfortable in the area of evangelism. "Oh, yes!" she responded, "I do it twice a week." Somehow it sounded more like taking her multiple vitamins. Evangelism is not just something you "do"—out there—and then get back to "normal" living. Evangelism involves taking people seriously, getting across to their island of concerns and needs, and then sharing that Christ is Lord in our natural context.

The problem stems, as I have said, from our great difficulty in believing that God is glorified in our utter humanity, rather than in our spiritually programmed responses. Most of us fear that who we are inside just is not enough. So we cover up our honest questions and doubts thinking they would not sound spiritual. Yet this means rejecting our humanness and thus losing our point of authentic contact with the world. We, of all people, should be offering the world a picture of what it means to be truly human. Yet it is often Christians who fear their humanity more than anyone else.

Just as there is confusion concerning what it means to be human, so is there confusion about what it means to be spiritual. We feel it is more spiritual to take our non-Christian roommate to a Bible study or to church than to a play or to a pizza parlor. Not only do we not understand our natural points of contact with the world, we do not understand our natural points of contact with God himself. He's the one who made us human beings in the first place. He is therefore interested in every aspect of our humanness. We dare not limit him to Bible studies and discussions with Christians. He created life and he desires to be glorified in the totality of all that adds up to life. And his power and presence will come crashing through to the world as we let him live fully in every aspect of our lives.

Our Model

Do we have any models for the kind of humanity God intended? Let's turn to the first whole human being who ever lived—Jesus Christ. He told us that as the Father sent him into the world, so he is sending us. How then did the Father send him? Essentially he became one of us. The Word became flesh. God did not send a telegram or shower evangelistic Bible study books from heaven or drop a million bumper stickers from the sky saying, "Smile, Jesus loves you." He sent a man, his Son, to communicate the message. His strategy has not changed. He still sends men and women—before he sends tracts and techniques—to change the world. You may think his strategy is risky—but that is God's problem, not yours.

In Jesus, then, we have our model for how to relate to the world—a model of vulnerability and identification. Jesus was a remarkably open man. He did not think it was unspiritual for him (fully realizing he was the Son of God) to share his physical needs (Jn. 4:7). He did not fear losing his testimony by asking for the emotional and prayerful support of his friends in the Garden of Gethsemane. Here is our model for genuine godliness—and we see him asking for support and desiring others to minister to him. We must learn then to relate transparently and vulnerably to others because that is God's style of relating to us. Jesus commands us to go and then preach—not to preach and then leave. We are not to shout the gospel from a safe and respectable distance and remain uninvolved. We must open our lives enough to let people see that we laugh and hurt and cry too. If Jesus left all heaven and glory to become one of us, shouldn't we at least be willing to leave our dorm room or Bible study circle to reach out to a friend?

How can we vulnerably and humanly relate to people in a way that will change the world? I think Jesus loved and changed the world in two ways: by his radical identification with men and women and by his radical difference. Jesus seemed to respond to people first by noticing what they had in common (Jn. 4:7). But it was often in the context of their similarities that Jesus' difference came crashing through (Jn. 4:10). It was as people discovered his profound humanness that they began to recognize his deity. God's holiness became shattering and penetrating as Jesus confronted people on his very own level of humanity. But the point is that it took both, his radical identification and his radical difference, to change the world. So it will be for us.

Collected Clues

If you are wanting to make contact with people

around you as a representative of Jesus Christ, here are some collected clues that may help.

1. *Be Yourself—Plus.* Let God make you fully you. Rejoice in your God-given temperament, and use it for God's purposes. God made some of us shy, others outgoing. We should praise him for that. If you are shy, remember that your shyness is not an excuse to avoid relationships—rather it is a means to love the world in a different way than an extrovert.

I get discouraged when I hear people say that it is easy for me to evangelize because I am outgoing. Being an extrovert *is not* the essential tool in evangelism—obedience and love are. There are many people I could never reach, and would probably only intimidate, because I am outgoing. God will have to use other Christians to reach them. But I do not feel guilty about it because I have learned that God is not glorified in my life with someone else's personality. I must be who I am created to be. And I must reach out to others in a way that is both sensitive to the person with whom I am talking and consistent with my own personality.

But regardless of our temperaments, we all must become initiators. More and more I see that the mark of mature Christians is whether they choose to be the "hosts" or the "guests" in relationships. Christians must be the ones who love, care and listen first. We can all take initiative, whether in a quiet or more conspicuous way.

2. *Be a Risk-Taker.* To take initiative opens us up to the risk of rejection. To let people inside our lives is a frightening but essential ingredient in evangelism. It is also a risk to leave our security blankets in order to penetrate *their* lives.

Recently I was walking through O'Hare Airport in Chicago when my purse slipped and everything tumbled out. As I was stuffing things back inside, a young woman with a baby stopped to ask the time. Then she nervously bit her lip and asked, "You don't know where I could get a drink, do you?" I didn't. But as I searched her face, I saw that she was distraught. So I stood up and started a conversation. She quickly interrupted with, "Do you know how much a drink would cost here?" I could see we were getting nowhere, and suddenly I heard myself saying, "Gee, I don't know, but would you like me to go with you to find the bar?" "Oh, would you? I would really love the company," she responded.

Off we went in search of a bar. And all the way I was kicking myself for it—going to a bar at noon with a perfect stranger. How unorthodox! Then I thought, "I wonder what Jesus would do in a situation like this?" I realized that he would probably be more concerned about *why* she needed the drink than about going into a bar. I knew that if I could not be at ease around her when she had a drink in her hand, and allow God to lead me into what *he* perceived as a mission field, then I would not be very effective in communicating God's unconditional love.

After we found the bar it took only minutes before she began sharing that she had decided to leave her husband. Her husband, unaware of her decision, would be meeting her at the airport in Michigan. She was petrified at facing his response and felt totally alone. "Oh, but it's ridiculous telling this to a complete stranger—how boring this must be for you," she would comment and then talked on.

The saddest part was her inability to believe anyone could care for her. She trusted no one. When at one point she mentioned a problem with which I told her I could identify, she said, "Oh, so that's why you act as if you care. Listen, aren't you afraid of picking up strangers like me? You really should be more careful." As I began to tell her who God was and that he was the one who brought me into situations like this, she seemed to hang on every word.

Soon we were walking to her plane, but I felt torn inside. I wanted to reach out to her and tell her how moved I was by her problems, and that there was a God who cared deeply for her. But she was so cold and defensive that I feared her rejection. Finally at the gate I took her hand and said, "Listen, I want you to know that I really care about you, and I'll be praying for you the minute you get off the plane." She just stared blankly at me. Then, turning away, she said, "Um . . . I'm sorry—I just don't know how to handle love," and walked away.

The encounter was not a smashing success, but I felt I was obedient. Being a Christian means taking risks: risking that our love will be rejected, misunderstood or even ignored. Now I am not suggesting that you race to your local bar for Jesus. But if you find yourself in a situation in which you believe God has put you, then accept the risk for his love's sake.

3. *See Beneath the Crust.* Once we have taken the risk and are in contact with a person, we must never assume that he or she won't be open to Christianity. Once we get beneath the surface of a person

we will usually discover a sea of needs. We must learn how to interpret those needs correctly, as Jesus did. Jesus was not turned off by needs—even needs wrongly met—because they told him something about the person.

The Samaritan woman had had five husbands and was currently living with a sixth man. The disciples took one look at her and felt, "That woman? Become a Christian? No way. Why, just look at her lifestyle!" But Jesus looked at the very same lifestyle and came to the opposite conclusion. What Jesus saw in her frantic male-hopping was not just a loose woman. It was not her human need for tenderness that alarmed Jesus, but rather the way she sought to meet that need. Even more, Jesus saw that her need indicated a real hunger for God. He seemed to be saying to the disciples, "Look at what potential she has for God. See how hard she is trying to find the right thing in all the wrong places."

That blows the lid right off evangelism for me. How many Samaritan men and women do you know? Everywhere I am, I see people frantically looking for the right things in all the wrong places. The tragedy is that so often my initial response is to withdraw and assume they will never become Christians. Yet God has shown me that they are usually the ones who are most open. We must ask ourselves: "How do I interpret the needs and lifestyles of my friends? Do I look at their drinking or drug habits or their sleeping around and say, 'That's wrong' and walk away? Or do I penetrate their mask and discover why they do this in the first place? And then do I try to love them where they are?"

We can show people that they are right to want to fill the void, and then they may be surprised by joy to discover that the emptiness inside is a "God-shaped vacuum."

4. *Avoid the "Holy Huddle Syndrome."* We must not become, as John Stott puts it, "rabbit-hole Christians." You know—the kind who pops his head out of the hole, leaves his Christian roommate in the morning and scurries to class, only to frantically search for a Christian to sit next to (an odd way to approach a mission field). Thus he proceeds from class to class. When dinner time comes, he sits with all the Christians in his dorm at one huge table and thinks, "What a witness!" From there he goes to his all-Christian Bible study, and he might even catch a prayer meeting where the Christians pray for the nonbelievers on his floor. (But what luck that he was able to live on the only floor

with seventeen Christians!) Then at night he scurries back to his Christian roommate. Safe! He made it through the day and his only contacts with the world were those mad, brave dashes to and from Christian activities.

What an insidious reversal of the biblical command to be salt and light to the world! The rabbit-hole Christian remains insulated and isolated from the world when he is commanded to penetrate it. How can we be the salt of the earth if we never get out of the saltshaker?

Christians, however, are not the only ones to blame for this phenomenon. The tragedy is that even the world encourages our isolationism. Have you ever wondered why everyone always "behaves" when the minister joins a television talk show? Suddenly their language changes and their behavior improves. Why? They want to do their part to keep the Reverend feeling holy. They will play the religious game while he is around because he needs to be protected from that cold, real world out there.

Sometimes non-Christians will act oddly around us because they are genuinely convicted by the Holy Spirit in us—and that is good. But all too often they are behaving differently because they feel that is the way they are supposed to act around religious types.

I am often put in a religious box when people discover what my profession is. Because I travel a great deal, I have a "clergy card" which enables me to travel at reduced rates. The only problem is that no one will ever believe I am authorized to use it! Somehow a young female just is not what the airline ticket agents have in mind when they see a clergy card. More than once I have been asked, "Okay, honey, now where did you rip this off?"

The funniest case occurred when I was flying from San Francisco to Portland. I arrived at the counter and was greeted by an exceedingly friendly male ticket agent.

"Well, hel-lo-o-o there!" he said.

"Uh . . . I'd like to pick up my ticket to Portland, please."

"Gee, I'm sorry—you won't be able to fly there tonight."

"Why—is the flight canceled?"

"No, it's because you're going out with me tonight."

"What?"

"Listen, I know this great restaurant with a hot band. You'll never regret it."

"Oh, I'm sorry, I really must get to Portland. Do you have my ticket?"

"Aw, what's the rush? I'll pick you up at 8:00. . . ."

"Look, I really must go to Portland," I said.

"Well, okay. Too bad though. Hey, I can't find your ticket. Looks like it's a date then!"

"Oh, I forgot to tell you, it's a . . . special ticket," I said.

"Oh, is it youth fare?"

"No, um, well, it's . . . ah, *clergy*," I whispered as I leaned over the counter.

He froze. "What did you say?"

"It's clergy."

"CLERGY!?!" he yelled, as the entire airport looked our way. His face went absolutely pale, and you could tell he was horrified by only one thought, "Oh no, I flirted with that nun!"

When he disappeared behind the counter, I could hear him whisper to the other ticket agent a few feet away, "Hey, George, get a load of that girl up there, she's *clergy*." Suddenly another man rose from behind the counter, smiled and nodded and disappeared again. Now I do not think I have ever felt so religious in my entire life. As I stood there trying to look as secular as possible, my ticket agent reappeared and stood back several feet behind the desk. Looking a bit shaken and sounding like a confused tape recording he said, "Good afternoon. We certainly hope there have been no inconveniences. And on behalf of Hughes Airwest, we'd like to wish you a very safe and pleasant flight . . . Sister Manley."

As humorous as this incident was, I think it shows how difficult it is to maintain our authenticity before the world. The challenge is to not allow ourselves to become more or less than human.

5. *Christians Are Positive!* Our attitude in responding to people is crucial. If you notice that non-Christians seem embarrassed, apologetic and defensive, it is probably because they are picking up *your* attitude. If you assume they will be absolutely fascinated to discover the true nature of Christianity, they probably will! If you communicate enthusiasm, not defensiveness, and carefully listen instead of sounding like a recording of "Answers to Questions You Didn't Happen to Ask," non-Christians will become intrigued. Learn to delight in all their questions—especially the ones you cannot answer. I often tell people I am very grateful that God is using them to sharpen me intellectually when I am stumped by a question. I tell them I do

not know the answer but I cannot wait to investigate it.

Learn also to identify with their defenses against Christianity. When talking with an intellectual professor, for example, we have every right to say, "I think one of the hardest issues a Christian must face is how in the world we know that it is true. Are we deluding ourselves and worshiping on the basis of need rather than truth?" In that way we can free non-Christians to feel at home with us. Walls are torn down and bridges built when we suggest the objections they may have.

Finally, approach relationships with non-Christians looking for ways in which God made you alike. Paul looked for points he had in common with others and began building from there (see Acts 17:22).

The girl who lives below me in my apartment house is a real swinger. She had just moved in, and every time I saw her she would be on her way to another party. We always exchanged friendly words and one day she said, "Becky, I like you. You're all right. Let's get together next week and smoke a joint, okay?" I replied, "Gee, thanks! I really like you too and I'd love to spend time with you. Actually I can't stand the stuff, but I'd sure love to do something else. See you later!"

Of course she looked a bit surprised, not so much because I did not smoke grass, but because I had expressed real appreciation at the thought of spending time with her. I could have told her, "I'm a Christian and I never touch the stuff," but I wanted to affirm whatever I possibly could first, without selling short the standards of a Christian. Too often we broadcast what we "don't do" when we should be trying to discover genuine points of contact.

6. *Put It All Together.* First, *investigate.* We need to learn how to be listeners first and proclaimers second. It is like rowing around an island, carefully studying the shoreline for an appropriate landing place. We explore our non-Christian friends' religious and family backgrounds, cultural interests, needs, dreams and fears. It is amazing to me that we spend fortunes so that missionaries can learn foreign languages while it never occurs to us that we must "learn the language" of our friends at home. We must get inside their thought forms and understand their questions. Don't leap to resolve every question; raise some! (God does that all the time in Scripture.)

Next, *stimulate.* Once we have some idea of who

we are talking to, we must learn to arouse their curiosity about the gospel. I think this is one of the most neglected aspects of evangelism. We try to saturate people with the light before we have caught their attention. In Acts 26:18 Paul says he was called *first* to open their eyes, *before* he helped them turn from darkness to light. He was called to arouse their interest so they would want to hear his message. We must learn to be "fishers of men" and not "hunters of men." We need to look at Paul and Jesus to study their fishing techniques.

Jesus was often deliberately vague and intrigued with people at first, not giving the whole answer until he had their complete interest. He knew that the Samaritan woman would not have a clue about what *living water* meant, any more than Nicodemus would comprehend the term *born again*. He was deliberately obscure to see if they had any spiritual interest and, if so, to enhance it. Paul aroused the curiosity of the Thessalonian Jews in the synagogue with his fierce logic and rational arguments. At Areopagus he captured the interest of the Greeks with his ability to use their secular poets to affirm his points. We too must develop a style of intriguing evangelism—not only through our conversation, but in our love for each other, our personal godliness and our genuine concern for non-Christians.

Finally, *relate*. Once we have discovered where people are and have aroused their interest in what we have to say, we are ready to relate the gospel message. Steps one and two are the necessary pre-evangelistic steps that will enable us to communicate Christ more effectively. But it is not enough to take the first two steps without the third. Paul, for example, knew his audience, found where they needed to grapple with commitment and then proclaimed the gospel (Acts 17:16-34).

Notice that Paul's message contained content and not just experience. Somehow it is difficult to imagine St. Paul on top of Areopagus defending his faith before secular philosophers by saying, "Gee, I dunno fellas, it's just this feeling in my heart." Our conversion experience may illustrate the power of the gospel, but it does not explain it. I cringe sometimes at the lack of content I hear when students are sharing their faith. Jesus begins to sound more like a happy pill to be popped, than a Lord to be obeyed at any cost.

Fully Human

We have discussed how we can identify with the

world as Jesus did. But Jesus also changed the world by his radical difference. How will our radical difference be expressed? The tension lies between identifying with the world and loving it as deeply as Jesus did (being similar to the world), and yet obeying the command "be ye therefore perfect" (being different from the world). We must remember that identification with the world does not equal being identical with the world. If we seek to understand the world but live exactly as non-Christians do, no impact will be made. Only as we identify with the world while living supernatural lives will revolution take place. That means our daily time alone with God will be critical to our evangelism, for it will change us into the likeness of Christ. Persistent prayer is equally vital—we must learn to love our friends enough to pray daily for them.

But I think our most radical difference will be felt when we live as we were created to be—fully human. Jesus has shown us that the most essential ingredient of true humanity is the freedom to respond totally, completely and passionately to God. If we let God make us authentic humans—not subcultural Christians, but affirming, vulnerable, open people who penetrate the world and love it as deeply as Jesus did—then the presence of God will be overwhelmingly felt by the world.

It cost God everything to identify with the nature of man. So will it cost us a great deal to identify with the nature of non-Christians. To give the message is easy. To give our lives is costly. But it is the giving of our lives that changes the world, for it authenticates the message that we preach. God asks for nothing less.

for further reading from InterVarsity Press

OUT OF THE SALTSHAKER
Rebecca M. Pippert writes a basic guide to evangelism as a natural way of life, emphasizing the pattern set by Jesus. paper, 192 pages; study guide, 12 studies

HOW TO GIVE AWAY YOUR FAITH
Paul Little offers suggestions on how to start a conversation, answer questions and call to commitment. paper, 131 pages

WHY AM I AFRAID TO TELL YOU I'M A CHRISTIAN?
Don Posterski shows how to win people to Christ by using Jesus' own approach: caring deeply about people as individuals and presenting the gospel in a way that matters to them. paper, 115 pages

BASIC CHRISTIANITY
John Stott's classic summary of the content of Christianity, covering who Christ is, what he has done, people's need in the face of sin and how they can respond to God. A great refresher for the believer and a clear presentation for the seeker. paper, 142 pages

SMALL GROUP EVANGELISM
Richard Peace outlines the principles of small group evangelism and provides exercises, Bible studies and role plays for training people to put the ideas into practice. paper, 240 pages

InterVarsity Press is only one aspect of the total ministry of Inter-Varsity Christian Fellowship. IVCF traces its spiritual foundations back to Cambridge University in 1877. Today more than 200 field staff members reach over 625 colleges and universities in the United States. The Nurses Christian Fellowship, a department of IVCF, has about 200 groups and active contacts in schools of nursing. The Student Missions Fellowship has 50 chapters in Bible colleges and other Christian schools. The Theological Students Fellowship, geared to seminary students, has nearly 1,000 subscribing members in this country.

The aim of students and faculty in IVCF is to present a strong evangelical witness on campus, to strengthen each other spiritually and to present the call of God to the foreign mission field. Each chapter is self-sustaining, self-governing and self-propagating.

To help students reach these goals, IVCF publishes, along with the InterVarsity Press titles, *HIS*, "the magazine of campus Christian living" and *The Nurses Lamp*, geared to the nursing profession. The multimedia branch of Inter-Varsity, TWENTYONE-HUNDRED, produces several presentations which aid students and staff in evangelism, discipleship and missions awareness.

IVCF is also affiliated with the IFES (International Fellowship of Evangelical Students) which links together the student movements in over 90 countries around the world. The IFES also offers resources of people, money and materials to countries just beginning their own indigenous movements.

For more information, write to IVCF, 233 Langdon, Madison, Wisconsin 53703.